CRUSHED AND SHATTERED BY OUR SCHOOL'S PRIZE-GIVING CEREMONIES

A Letter From a Learner to Bosabethu Secondary School

By Dr Hlabathi Maapola-Thobejane

COPYRIGHT AND PUBLISHING

CRUSHED AND SHATTERED BY OUR SCHOOL'S PRIZE GIVING CEREMONIES

By Dr Hlabathi Maapola-Thobejane

Print ISBN: 9780620808033

eISBN: 9780359912735

Layout, eBook conversion and online distribution by
www.bulabuka.co.za

CONTENTS

DEDICATION

This book is dedicated to the following people:

1. My parents: Paul and Gladys Maapola, for having laid a very strong foundation in all areas of my life. You are the best…!
2. My late first-born son, Thato. You have left a void in my heart that can never be filled. May your soul rest in peace!

ABOUT THE BOOK

The book comes in a form of a letter written by a Grade 12 learner who decided to reflect on their school's prize-giving ceremonies. The learner (Lebone), is doing Grade 12 and she is feeling so discouraged to study because of the following reasons:

- Despite having studied very hard since grade 8, she has never received an academic award at the school because there were always those that teachers selected for the awards at the end of each year.
- Her parents do not trust that she will succeed at tertiary institutions because she has never received an academic award at school.
- The neighbours and the community label her as the stupid girl. They say Lebone has never made her parents proud by making them attend the prize-giving ceremonies like what other girls did to their parents in the neighbourhood.

Lebone is so disheartened and she decided to interview other learners to check how they feel about their school's prize-giving ceremonies. Scenarios that show how diverse learners (those that receive and those that do not receive) become negatively affected by these ceremonies are highlighted in the book.

As she was interviewing other learners at the school, she was referred to a learner (Mmakgabo) who was once at the same school. Mmakgabo used to get most of the awards at school and was known by everyone at school and in the neighbourhood to be scooping all the awards every year. Unfortunately, Mmakgabo did not make it at tertiary institutions and she was back at home and very miserable. During the interview, Mmakgabo shared her life encounters at tertiary institutions and the damage that the academic awards she used to get at the school contributed to her failure in life.

As a result, Mmakgabo's ordeal motivated Lebone to go back and study, to trust herself, to continue working very hard and to disregard what other people say about her. She is also motivated to have seen that; not receiving an academic award at school is not a ticket to failure in life as her society puts it. In the same way, Lebone also learnt that, in the same manner, getting academic awards every year at school is also not a ticket for one's success in future. In summary, the book shows two sides of how prize-giving ceremonies crush and shatter children:

    – **Lebone – who has never received an academic award at school.**

She was crushed and shattered by the prize-giving ceremonies at school and at home, from the preparatory stage until when the day is being celebrated. At school, her friends were excited and talking about the upcoming ceremony. At home, her two siblings who always received the awards were always the topic and she was ignored. The community was also blaming her and telling her that she will be a failure in future.

- **Mmakgabo – the former learner who used to scoop all the academic awards but did not make it at tertiary institutions.**

She was crushed and shattered by the school's prize-giving ceremonies. Teachers and parents have put too much pressure on her to do Medicine. Although she was not coping, the intelligent girl label that was accorded to her during her school years made it difficult for her to accept that she was not coping. She was afraid and also jealousy to participate in group discussions. She started lying about her results and her life became a mess in all areas.

ABOUT BOSABETHU SECONDARY SCHOOL

Bosabethu Secondary School is a school in one of the provinces of South Africa. The school is well known by everyone in the community for its outstanding general image. The management and the school governing body's systems have been well thought of in a way that it is all systems go at the school. Teachers are doing their work as best as they can. Learners are disciplined and do their school work with great vigour and zeal. As a result, the school is always producing outstanding Grade 12 results.

ABOUT THE AUTHOR

Dr Hlabathi Maapola-Thobejane was born on the 28th August 1972 in Saulsville (Pretoria-Gauteng Province) and bred in a rural village of Ga-Mashashane in the Capricorn District (Limpopo Province), South Africa. She started teaching in 1993 when she was 20 years of age.

During her tenure in the Department of Basic Education, she occupied all levels of the teaching fraternity:

- a teacher
- an acting departmental head
- a deputy principal
- a principal of a township secondary school.

She taught at primary schools, secondary schools, at a special school and at a full-service school in both rural and urban areas.

She worked for JET Education Services as a Technical Advisor for Teaching and Learning on the TVET college improvement project. She also worked at the National Department of Basic Education as a Technical Advisor for Care and Support Teaching and Learning (CSTL) in the Technical Support Directorate.

She has trained teachers, education specialists, lecturers and speech therapists on inclusive education in all nine provinces of

South Africa for the Department of Basic Education, Macmillan Education, University of Limpopo, UNISA and WITS University.

She has been a lecturer at the University of Limpopo. Currently, she is a lecture at UNISA, in the Department of Inclusive Education.

FOREWORD

Many, if not all schools organise prize-giving ceremonies towards the end of each year. The question is: how often do schools make an effort to review how these ceremonies are being organised, managed and celebrated? During these ceremonies, excellence in different categories is being recognised and learners go home with outstanding awards. Unfortunately, it is not all of them who get an award on the day. Therefore, although the day has been earmarked to celebrate learners' excellence, it is only a handful of learners whose excellence is being celebrated on that day in many schools.

We all know that each and every learner is unique and special. They are special in their own way and all of them want to grow, to develop and to succeed. Schools should be institutions where all learners, diverse as they are, feel safe and cared for. Schools are meant to empower all learners, not just the chosen few. An essential skill of the 21st century is that people should be able to collaborate. Therefore, for them to all achieve, they are made to work together and support one another in classrooms.

Are prize-giving ceremonies creating a safe and caring environment for them to work together? Is it not a fact that schools need to encourage all of them to: hard work, develop, take risks and see failure as a learning process? Do the schools take time and reflect on whether their year-end practice promote individual learners or enhance the culture of working together? Why is it that our schools have turned into institutions that are very good in categorising and classifying learners instead? To make matters worse, parents and the whole community also support these ceremonies by honouring invitations. As a result, they also classify their children as intelligent, clever or stupid.

Why do we define learners by awards? We keep on telling them that they are all equally important to the school and to parents, yet, at the end of the year, there are some that become more important than others. Let us go through this letter that I took time to write; let us hear what learners of Bosabethu Secondary School have to say about their school's prize-giving ceremonies. Hopefully, at the end, schools and the whole society can consider reviewing their practices and start thinking of alternative ways that embrace and celebrate diversity so that all learners could feel equally important and valued at schools and at home.

CHAPTER 1

Dear Bosabethu Secondary School

My name is Lebone. I regard myself as the fortunate one because I am able to put down my thoughts so that everyone can read. I have been a learner at Bosabethu Secondary School for up to four years now. I started here with Grade 8. This year I am in grade 12 and I will not be coming back next year. This is the reason why I have decided to write this letter.

I take this moment to write this letter to you in love. This letter comes from the bottom of my heart. Take your time and read what I have to say about the school. Sometimes the good things that we think we do to others ruin their lives forever without us realising exactly where we have gone wrong. This is what is happening with the school. The culture that has been created at the school is the one that everyone thinks it prioritises teaching and learning because everyone knows what to do and at what time. As a result, parents from the neighbourhood and far want their children to be admitted at the school. Unfortunately, available resources always limit the school to admit a set number. Despite the good work that the school is doing, the excellent systems that have been put, outstanding results that are being produced at the school, ONE STONE REMAINS UNTURNED.

I have come to realise; this stone is the misery that contributes immensely to all the ills that have befallen our beloved country. I never knew that, the reason why marriages are breaking up is solely because of this stone. The reason our youth are abusing drugs and alcohol is because of this stone. The reason why the society no longer cares about what the next person feels is because of this stone. This stone is the reason why our streets are filled with drop-outs that ultimately perpetuate the level of crime. It is because of this stone that my child remains my child and no longer your child or our child.

Why then are we so quiet? Why do we keep on pretending everything is fine? Do we really have to continue like this? No ways, we all know what is happening at Bosabethu. Enough is enough! Bosabethu, we are coming out into the open! We know what you are doing. **Your prize-giving ceremonies are a concern!** The damage you have done is immeasurable and irreversible, and you have to be brought to book for all what you continue doing, year after year. It has to stop and it has to stop now! The question that lingers on is whether you are aware of the massive damage you continue to cause on our society. Is it a deliberate or unconscious effort? Go back to the drawing board, but first, for you to do that, you first have to travel this journey with me for you to understand the damage you have caused and continue to do to our society.

I am writing this letter because I do not wish anybody to travel the path that I have travelled. It has been a thorny and scary one on the inside. However, a pleasurable, gratifying and prestigious one on the outside. Unfortunately, the outside will be washed away by the winds, the storms and the rain. But, the inside will remain with me for as long as I live. The inside will be that part of me I will be reliving for as long as I am on this planet earth. The inside will torment, haunt and frustrate me forever. The inside will define me because it has now become part of me.

It is unfortunate that I see a lot of my schoolmates travelling this path with me in silence. This silence brings a total shut-down. This silence makes what is unbearable to seem bearable. It is not only my schoolmates that are aware and travelling this rocky journey with me. Even my parents are aware and they are also travelling this journey in silence with me. All what they do is to succumb and suffer in silence. All what they do is to try very hard to cope with the ordeal until they run out of alternatives. How could they allow this to happen to me? What I am thinking is that they have also travelled this route and they regard it as the normal way of doing things.

But how do you call this the normal way of doing things? Is it because you are scared of standing out and tarnish your dignity and image? If that is what you are thinking, then you must know that, it may be true, you are winning in maintaining your dignity and image but, to the detriment of my future. Not only my future, but the future of the society as a whole. This usually amazes me; I do not understand why people choose to keep quiet about this. Could it be because they have been taught to keep quiet and persevere even when things are not going well? Could it be that they have been taught that silence is golden?

I don't think so, no ways. This is my life. What is happening around me has everything to do with me. What is happening around me has to make sense to me. What is happening around me, especially when it comes from the school environment, has to be what I am able to handle, not what makes me feel alien. It can never be alien to me but stays with me. If it is alien to me, then it is not meant for me. Let it go to those who would be comfortable with it, not with me. But who will be comfortable with this? Who will be able to stand this? I do not think any learner from whatever part of the country would ever feel comfortable with this. It is not a good experience; it does not bring good memories. It is nerve-wracking, it brings goose-bumps, it is hair-rising and it is nail-biting. It needs to be reconsidered because all what it does to us is harm. It is a silent killer. It is killing us; it is destroying us. For how long, for how long do we have to suffer this anomaly in silence? It has caused enough damage. Let it find its place somewhere, not here, not here among us.

CHAPTER 2

Bosabethu, there is only one question that I have for you. The question is: Are all learners valued at your school? Do you celebrate and embrace diversity? Who are you awarding a prize at the end of the year? I hope these questions sit well with you because you are organizing prize-giving ceremonies year after year. Year in, year out, you go all out to make sure this event is organised at the school and that it eventually becomes a success.

You start by budgeting for this event. You make us contribute towards the big day. You raise funds for this occasion. Eventually, you agree on the date, time and the venue for the celebration. You identify the categories that you are going to award prizes; I hope you do all that in advance. You give teachers the responsibility of identifying learners who match the categories you have worked out in their classes. What once made me wonder how the process was being managed was when I was doing Grade 10.

The identification was haphazardly made during the week of the ceremony. I saw teachers coming to our classes and identifying learners who qualify for some of the categories like cleanliness. What bothered me was that the identification was made without involving us as learners. I said to myself: How could one person, a teacher, decide on such a serious matter, about us, without us?

The sad part is that for the past four years at this school, I tried very hard to qualify for an academic award in at least one subject. This has not started now; it started when I was still at a primary school. Year in, year out, the same learners were being awarded for performing well in different subjects. I fought, fought very hard. I denied myself hours of sleep as well as my favourite TV programmes. I missed out on Sunday church services. I did not go to malls with my family and friends whenever they were going out. All what I wanted was to make my mother proud. I wanted her to attend the prize-giving ceremony at the end of the year like other parents.

I wanted this to happen because my mother was working very hard to make sure that she provided us with everything that we needed to do our schoolwork properly. We know as her children that she was not earning much. We sometimes struggled to get fashion clothes we needed like our friends. However, she told us that she might sometimes not have the money to buy clothes and pizzas for us, but, she would always have the money to buy school stuff. Indeed, whenever there was a school project and we needed to buy the project's material, money was always available.

This was the reason why I so much wanted to make my mother happy. Like other parents, she wanted us to succeed. Not only to succeed, but to succeed beyond expectations. She always told us that if we want to succeed in life, we were to strive to be the best in everything that we did. As a result, in all the years, I knew I was not her favourite because she never attended a single prize-giving ceremony where I would have been awarded a prize for academic excellence. She only attends when I receive a prize for extra-curricular activities. I know, she does not like this. But what must I do? This is the question that I have been asking myself all these school years.

I wish I could have had a clue of what I had to do to make her proud. I wish I could have known what I had to do to make her smile. I wish I could have had an idea what I had to do so that like all other parents, she could have attended the ceremony to feel the joy and amusement of seeing her child receiving an academic award. I know this would have been her pride and would have also made her feel worthwhile. I am saying this because I had seen parents sharing invitations they had received from the school with families, friends and colleagues.

It kills me to think that my mother has never felt what other parents feel until today. This make me feel like a failure, it makes me feel incomplete, and it makes me feel worthless, useless and stupid. It makes me wish to be someone else; it makes me wish to have what others have. It feels like I do not have what other children have. As a result, it makes me wonder, will I make it at tertiary institutions next year? I am so discouraged; I am so powerless. This has tarnished my self-image; my self-esteem is so low because of this. I have never received an academic award in my entire school life. This makes me to question my existence.

But why do I sometimes wish to be someone else? Why do I sometimes feel ashamed of myself? Why do I sometimes feel sorry about being myself? Why do I sometimes feel I am incomplete? Why do I sometimes feel as if nobody cares about how I feel? This is because of the pressure I find myself in. Nobody talks about me during the time of prize-giving ceremonies. Nobody talks to me during this time I hate most, the time of prize-giving ceremonies. During this time, it is like I am non-existent.

Everywhere you go during this period; all talks are about the son of so and so who received a lot of awards. Everywhere you go will be about the daughters of so and so who are making their parents proud. I sometimes feel as if I can dig a hole and bury myself in there and would come out once the period had passed. It becomes so painful, so painful that I find very difficult to cope. It becomes so unbearable, so unbearable that one would not want to be seen.

There is something strange that I have noticed. What I have realised is that I am in this pain by myself. Nobody seems to care; my friends at school do not care about me because they are so fortunate that they always get prizes. All what they do is sit around and compare the different prizes they have received whilst I stand on the side watching them. Even when I go to them, I find them so engrossed in the celebration mood that they disregard my presence. That hurts me, it hurts me so much and, unfortunately, I have to be there every time, year after year and watch this.

Another thing that I have noticed is that teachers turn to forget about my presence during this time. They take all of their attention and put it on learners that will receive prizes. They call the lists and hand out parents' invitation letters while they ignore me because there will not be a prize for me. I do not know if they ignore me deliberately or if they just do not have time to think about me during this period. This haunts me; it haunts me in a way that I feel pierced. Unfortunately, I do not even have the guts to ask my teachers why. I once thought of asking them, but, eventually, I just thought I was going to hurt myself even more if they would not put any effort into addressing what I am going through.

As if that is not enough, when I go home, it gets worse. It gets worse because I have two siblings, I am the eldest, but, year after year they get awards at school. Therefore, every time when I am supposed to go home during this period, I am always unsettled to sit with the family. I become uneasy because the topic of prize-giving ceremonies could just creep in anytime. As a result, every time when I am with the family during this time, I would just quietly say my short silent prayers hoping that the topic would not arise. It could become very difficult and frustrating at times.

To my surprise, I think the society does not see this in the same way. The society does not seem to be sharing the same sentiment with me. It seems to be fine with the whole arrangement. Instead, I think all what they see in me is that foolish girl who does not want to make her parents proud. All what they see in me is that girl who is very lazy to read. I don't think that individual difference is being valued by the society at large. If it was valued, the issue of prize-giving ceremonies could have long been realigned to suit all of us. Unfortunately, unlike me, whose parents have given up on, other parents are putting pressure on their children. Children are being put under such pressure that they sometimes find it very difficult to cope.

I once overheard my classmates sharing their predicament of being recipients' year after year. One of them said: "My dad is never happy about my performance, when I get 80%, he wants 90% and when I get 90% he wants 100%. This is just too much; I do not think he is being fair to me". This has made me realise that, for as much as I think they are better off as compared to me; the pressure they experience is so drastic. As I continued to listen to their conversation, the other one was saying: "You know what, my mother has promised to buy me an expensive cell-phone if I manage to be the best student in Mathematics, she also promised to give me a clothing voucher on top of that. Please guys, I have to get this".

As I was listening, I realised that the issue of prize-giving ceremonies is worse than I thought. This I noticed when I heard the other one saying: "I know for sure that I am going to be the overall best student in all subjects. I discussed that with my parents from the beginning of the year, we have invested everything in that; they paid for my extra-lessons, they also hired full-time private tutors in all subjects for me, so, I don't have a reason not to outshine all of you guys". It was during this moment that beads of sweat on my forehead began to show. I started thinking how the person who was talking had been in class throughout the year? She never wanted to share information with the rest of the group. She never wanted to contribute an idea when we were put in groups.

What kinds of values are being instilled in her, selfishness and pride? This I thought because of the pride she displayed as she was expressing herself. With pride she was confidently saying she would not be outshone by anyone. With pride she was saying she was the best, and with pride she was saying nobody could challenge her. As a result, for me to get different perspectives of what I regarded as the ordeal at our school, I decided to find out what other learners of Bosabethu Secondary School felt about this practice of prize-giving ceremonies. The following chapter outlines their different perspectives of prize-giving ceremonies.

CHAPTER 3

I decided to use my time fruitfully by conducting interviews during lunch and after school. My wish to accomplish my vision made me think of finding out what other learners felt about the issue at hand. I decided that I was not going to ask for permission from anyone because I did not know whether what I was doing will be approved by the school authorities or not. As a result, on my own, I decided that I would do it behind the scenes. The aim was not to destroy the image of my school, but, to uncover the ills that hampered the success and happiness of most of the children at the school.

I then decided to use my cell-phone to record the interviews that I conducted with learners that I randomly selected. I transcribed our conversations while I was alone at home. Before I interviewed my learners, I told them that my aim was simply to know how different learners felt about prize-giving ceremonies. I told them that their views might be published but their identities would not be revealed. As a result, names that have been used are not their real names. Only one question was put to all learners that were interviewed and that was: "What is your opinion on prize-giving ceremonies that are being organised at our school every year? "Leaners at the school had this to say:

Gladstone

One thing that I am sure of is that I am going to receive a lot of prizes like I always do. You see, this is my last year at this school and you know, from Grade 8, I have been receiving a lot of them. I wish you can go with me to my home and see for yourself. I no longer know where to hang them. They are hung all over in the house, my mother took some to her office and my father took some to his office as well. But, you won't believe, I still have a lot of them that are just lying in the drawers. They are even accumulating dust. It is just unfortunate because they have my name on, if that was not the case, I was simply going to give them to other learners who never got an opportunity to be awarded a prize, just like you.

I am telling you, these certificates no longer have meaning to all of us in my family. They are many; so many that they are just adding to trash. The trophies as well, are so many that they are just making our displays cluttered. I sometimes wonder if these people are aware about how I feel. I don't want these things anymore. If I had a choice, I would tell them to give them to other learners who will value them.

We were talking about them last night as I was telling them that we have started preparing for this year's ceremony. My father was saying maybe we should go for a holiday on the day so that I do not come with more of the clutter. But, my mother said that would not be fair to the school. I do not understand why we have to be fair to the school when the school itself is not being fair about how they waste their financial resources. They had better start awarding other learners. I wish I had some couple years left at the school so that I could raise that with teachers, maybe they would listen. I do not want these papers that they keep bombarding me with saying I am the best. I am not the best. Many tasks that I submitted are a joint effort; we do them together as a group, so why do they single me out of the rest of the group at the end of the year? I do not like it.

Balesanyana

My name is Balesanyana. This is my first year at Bosabethu Secondary School. I do not have much to say about how they conduct their prize-giving ceremonies as you are asking. However, if you do not mind, I can share with you how the primary school that I am coming from do theirs. It is the primary school close-by, the one that feeds this school with Grade 8 learners. I started my Grade R at that primary school. In Grade R, we were all given certificates and the same presents at the end of the year, all of us. It felt very good; I can still describe how I felt that day. All of our parents were invited. Things started changing when I was doing Grade 1. However, I was so fortunate to receive a few certificates at the end of the year. On that day, it was many of us who got awarded certificates. I think it was almost more than half of the Grade 1 learners. I think all parents were invited and it felt very good. As they were calling names of learners that were receiving awards, numbers started decreasing as we were proceeding with the upper grades. I still remember one parent who was seated next to me saying, it is getting tougher and tougher now, only the cleverest ones will receive in the higher grades. That did not feel good to me, and as few learners were being called to receive the certificates, I thought, the parent was correct. It means it is only those who are clever that are getting the certificates as we progress through the grades. That thinking got engrained in my mind. Every year it kept on lingering in my mind when prize-giving ceremonies kept on attesting to what was in my mind and that was: only the cleverest ones will receive awards in the higher grades.

Indeed, few learners got the awards in the higher grades every year during my entire stay at the primary school. Those learners that got the awards received a number of them in different subjects. It was only a few of them, up to three learners in each grade. They were sharing certificates amongst themselves. I still remember a certain Grade 7 boy who got certificates in all subjects. He was also awarded for cleanliness and another category that I could not remember. Unfortunately, with me, that award that I got in Grade 1 was the last for my entire primary school years. No matter how hard I tried to work, there were always those who performed better than me according to the teachers. Those are the ones who were already in the good books of our teachers. That is what I thought and decided to make peace with. As a result, year in, year out, we all knew learners that were going to be awarded before they could even be awarded on the actual day.

Once again, the whole practice made me believe that as one progresses through the grades, things get tougher and tougher at school and it was only the clever ones that would survive and succeed. The question that remained with me up to today was: did it then means the few that received awards were the only ones that would survive schooling? As for the rest of us, we were just going to school for the sake of it, not that we would succeed, but only because we had to. We cannot sit at home; we have to go to school. It is a system, you are born, you go to school, you go to church, then you will either drop-out of school, go to a university or go and look for employment and then you die; a vicious system.

Ledjadji

I am doing Grade 9 at this school. Last year I got three awards in English, Natural Science and Life Orientation. Although I was happy to receive the awards, that was not what I expected. I expected more and my parents were equally disappointed. They tried so hard not to show their disappointment, but, I know my father, I know how he reacts when he is disappointed, that frown is what I saw on him that day.

When I was at primary school, I used to receive not less than five certificates every year. They were so used to it; I am used to it as well. To tell the truth, I totally do not have an idea of what happened last year. I stayed at home and studied the way I used to study. One thing I remembered was that during the year, there were about three teachers that always wanted us to clean the classroom and I told them I was not going to do that. I think, they hate me because I refused to carry out their instructions.

When I go to school, I go there to study. I do not go there to clean the yard, the classrooms and the toilets. They compromise our study time. They need to consider hiring people for the upkeep of the school. My mother told me that I needed to make sure that I used every minute that I had to study.

Even when I am at home, I only wash the dishes that I have used. That is because, I must not waste time with household chores, I am not a maid, but a school child. Let maids do their work and learners do theirs. The thing is, my parents want me to get as many certificates as possible at the end of the year. That is the reason they do everything in their power not to distract me so that I am able to concentrate on my school work. What I am sure of is that, this year I will get a number of them.

Phomolo

I am doing grade 11. To tell the truth, I have never received any certificate in my entire school years. I have given-up. I know for sure that even this year, I will not get anything. When they start arranging for the day I simply switch off and concentrate on other things. I am on the school choir. What I hate most is that they always put us on the programme on that day to entertain the visitors.

I love music very much, so I just come and become part of the choir on that day because of my love for music. If it was not for that, I was simply going to stay at home and do other things like what most of my classmates do. They do that, the prize-giving ceremony day is a holiday for them. They stay at home and nobody has ever said a word about that. So it means, staying at home on the day is not a problem.

Another thing that I do not like about the day is that, as they prepare for the day, they give us requests for donations circulars. We go all around to our families, in our neighbourhood, in our churches and everywhere looking for money. We are told that money is being used to buy things that will be needed on that day. What I have noticed is that those that normally go all out looking for donations and ultimately come with a lot of money are those that will never receive a single award. What they get is a 'thank you' from teachers for having collected a huge sum of money.

Is that fair? They use our energy and our time and make us go around looking for donations. Teachers also do that; they go around asking for donations just for a handful of learners. If all that initiative was meant to celebrate all learners at the school, then I would be saying something different. Another thing that I have noticed is that all school programmes come to a halt during the period of prize-giving ceremonies. Do we really need to compromise other things that benefit the entire school population because of just a handful of learners? The other unpleasant aspect of it again is that the same people receive the awards year in, year out. We already know them. I don't mean to envy them, but I think there are better things that we could be focusing on other than to waste time on those prize-giving ceremonies that tend to focus on particular learners.

Obenathe

My name is Obenathe. I am doing Grade 10 at Bosabethu Secondary School. I do not know whether teachers take time to reflect and review how they do these prize-giving ceremonies. You do not have to ask further about how we feel as learners at this school about these ceremonies. I am saying this because we even avoid talking about them amongst ourselves when we are together as learners and when we are with our teachers in our classes.

We avoid talking about them because we are two groups; those that receive and those that do not receive. Some occasionally receive and they do not even know where to put themselves. As a result, because they are never sure, the topic makes them feel restless and they do not want to talk about it. I do not know where to start, but, in short, prize-giving ceremonies are a nuisance at this school. They are not fairly organised, there is favouritism; it is a matter of who you know as a learner. It is a matter of in whose good books you are as a learner. Some male teachers go to an extent of sleeping with these girls so that they could be awarded prizes at the end of the year.

I do not think that the principal knows about this. Another thing that is disgusting about these ceremonies is that they classify us as clever and stupid. Are we really stupid? All of us, 99% of the school? If that is the case then, let them close down this school. Why do they keep on segregating us, we said 'apartheid' was not a good system, yet we are practicing it here? You know very well because this is your school as well. How teachers treat these learners that get prizes is totally different from how they treat all of us. They are special!

I hate this day; I hope you remember what happened last year. I am not sure if they will do the same thing this year. I am referring to when they decided to centralise the ceremony by bringing the whole circuit in that nearby hall. Do you still remember? Imagine, twenty-four secondary schools going to a central venue. Each school brought their children. Again, do you remember how painful that was to us who could not go to the hall? It was only learners who were going to be awarded who were invited with their parents. They were so excited; here at school they hired common transport for them and their parents.

I still remember when we were gazing at them as they were getting into that bus. They got in, with our teachers. We were left standing here without a word to either say, go home or get into your classes. It was so painful; we were so quiet, the whole school, watching. After the bus left, most of us also left and went home. You do not have an idea of what happened to me on that day. As we were going home, we met one of our teachers at the gate and he said: You stupid people...! Go home, your friends have gone to receive awards because they also listen to their teachers. I was so pissed off; it was so painful. I do not think that teacher has an idea of the damage he has caused on me that day.

When I reached home, my grandmother asked me why I was back that early. I cannot blame her for having asked, she had to. Unfortunately, I could not tell her the truth because I immediately thought about what the teacher said to us, that we were stupid. I had to feign illness; I told her they had released me because of a terrible headache. The poor old lady offered some pills; I only took the pills she offered knowing very well that I was not going to take them. As a result, I had to spend the whole day in bed on that day. I was so dejected in spirit that I could not even open my books. That is the life we had to be used to at this school. Is it fair? I do not think they are being fair to us. I do not know whether they are still going to centralise the ceremony again this year or whether it will be held here at school. But, even if they do it here at school, to tell the truth; that ceremony is a torture to us who never receive any awards on the day despite of efforts we put in our studies. But what can we do, what can we say? It will come and go. We just have to be strong and it will pass like it always did.

CHAPTER 4

The information I gathered during the interviews with some of the learners made me realise the extent to which most of us are so crushed and shattered by these prize-giving ceremonies. Eventually, different perspectives I got from these learners made me think about a certain lady who used to live in our neighbourhood. That lady did her secondary schooling at our same school and her name was Mmakgabo. Mmakgabo was known by everyone in our community because she used to have it all. She got the 'intelligent girl' label from everyone because she received awards from when she started at primary until high school. For that, everyone at school knew that she would collect all the certificates that were available in different categories. Nobody competed her, and everyone knew that. That honour and label she had been accorded made me to think of organising an interview session with her to get her view of prize-giving ceremonies. Fortunately, as I was striving to get her contact number, one of the teachers who taught her gave it to me and I secured an appointment with her.

It was on a Saturday morning when I went to meet Mmakgabo as agreed telephonically. I went to where she was staying; a two-roomed house with patches of zinc at the back; it looked like the builders ran out of bricks while they were still building. She took me into the house where we together sat on a chair that looked like it was once a sofa. It was so hoary, so overused that they even decided to put wood on it so that people could sit.

Without wasting time, I introduced myself to her. I told her I had come from the neighbourhood and that I was a Grade 12 learner at Bosabethu Secondary School. As I was introducing myself, she looked straight into my eyes without a blink. I continued, told her that the reason I had come to her was to share my frustrations and experiences of being a learner at that school. I told her that I was so frustrated that, no matter how hard I tried to work and denied myself the entertainments that teenagers enjoy, I still could not manage to get myself a single award like other girls.

I told her the experiences that were caused by my frustrations. That, everyone has lost hope in me; I am not trusted by my parents and relatives that I will pass my final exams; my own mother even told me that even if I got a pass by luck, unlike my friends, I would not manage at tertiary institutions. My own mother told me that, when she looked at me, she saw someone who would end up dropping-out of school and giving birth to many children so that I could depend on their child-support grant. That got into me, especially because it is true I have never received a merit award. It is true that; as compared to my friends and peers, nobody has trust in me in the whole family and neighbourhood. I told Mmakgabo that the only thing that kept me going was that, no matter how everyone thought of me, I told myself that I was just going to keep on pushing very hard and I will never lose hope or give up on myself. Mmakgabo was just quiet looking at me as I was narrating my predicament. All what she did as I was speaking was to nod or shake her head. I did not know what she was thinking of me, until when she said to me at last: Ok, I hear your story Lebone, but tell me now, what brought you here?"

I was happy that she said a word at last, and then I told her exactly what brought me to her. I told her that I came to her because of the good name she had made for herself at our school and in the whole community. Everyone refer to her whenever they want to motivate or blame their kids for not performing well at school which results in them not receiving merit awards at the end of the year. Every parent wants her children to be exactly like her during their school years. As I was saying all that, unlike before when I was telling her about me, this time, Mmakgabo was looking down. With her arms folded, she was looking down without even attempting to nod or shake her head like before. The thought that she was not enjoying listening to how everyone sees her did not ring a bell. She kept on looking down; I kept on showering her with compliments.   At last, she stood and looked at me, she was in tears.

She looked at me, wept bitterly until I hugged her and tried to sit her down. She wept so much that all my attempts to cool her down did not succeed. I was so much in trouble that I did not know what to do anymore as she continued crying. At last, I decided to take a mug and went outside and draw water from a drum that I noticed at the corner of the house as I was coming in. As I was going out, Mmakgabo did not stop crying. Suddenly, I came back and tried to make an effort of making her drink water.

I could feel the cooling effect that was brought by the water as she was drinking. I held the mug for her as she was drinking non-stop until the last drop. I then decided to go and fill the mug again, this time she managed to drink for a while and then stopped as she was breathing heavily. At that time, I tried to wipe her face with a cloth that was in my bag. Eventually, she cooled down, and kept quiet for some time. I was so patient with her and I also decided to keep quiet and not ask her a thing. Eventually, she said to me: Lebone, if I had it my way; if I could turn back the clock, the only thing I would do would have been to reverse all the so-called merit awards that I was fooled with during my school years. I was so surprised at the words she uttered that I did not understand what she meant. My astonished gaze made her realise that I was indeed confused and did not understand what she meant.

She then sat down, held my hand and started narrating her story. She told me that: she hated herself so much today because of the awards she used to receive; she was a failure in life because of the prizes she was getting when she was at school; she lived like a hobo because of the prizes she was receiving; she does not associate herself with anyone today because of the prizes she used to receive; she lost her marriage because of the awards she used to get; her two sons turned their back on her and chose to live with their father because of the awards that she received; she is not accepted within the community she lived in because of the prizes she used to receive at Bosabethu Secondary School.

The confusion and amazement in me got even worse as she was talking. I was trying to make sense of what she implied but I hardly made meaning of what she was saying. She went on: sometimes the good things that we think we do to people harm them immensely without us realising the damage we are causing or have caused. I was very surprised at that, again trying to make sense of what she meant, but all attempts to understand her did not succeed.

She went on: I wonder if the whole society is aware of the damage they have caused on me. Is the principal aware? I doubt it. Are the teachers there aware? I doubt it. Are learners at the school aware of the damage they have caused on me? I am not sure, but I doubt it. I doubt it because like you are saying, the school still continue to destroy the lives of more and more children. Those that are still getting these prizes year in year out are not even aware of the damage that may be caused by that. But, believe me, as they venture in life, they will come to realise that at that school, nobody could have been made to have it all while others are left desperate.

As she was saying this, though I had a lot of things that I felt I could ask for clarity, I decided to allow her state her case without any disruptions. She went on: You know Lebone, I know that you may not understand what I mean by all this, but one day, you will be able to make sense of it. Another thing that I have noticed is that members of our society continue to be misled by the schools. They are being misled because they still believe that a child who gets a lot of awards during her school years is bound to succeed in life. With that misconception, they continue to put their children under pressure. They expect so much more than what children could offer. But, I cannot blame them; the practice at Bosabethu Secondary School is the same at most of our schools globally. It has become a way of life and nobody is saying anything about it.

She continued: Lebone, you need to consider yourself auspicious, consider yourself propitious. I did not have an idea of how it feels to be written-off by everyone around you until now. My advice to you is: instead of seeing yourself as a failure today, choose to see yourself as a success tomorrow. You are going to succeed Lebone, you are going to make it in life. I am saying all this because as I was listening to you when you were saying everyone has written you off expect for yourself, I had goose bumps all over my body. I celebrated; I celebrated because I have learnt to believe that, I do not have to win the world through external convictions of any kind for me to win and succeed in life. The only thing that I need to succeed in life is to believe in myself and my God. Affirmations from others have a way of deceiving people.

I am saying this because I have learnt the hard way. I so much relied on the public opinion in everything I did with my life in a way that I ended up losing it. I still remember my school years very well. Every day when I woke up, I took all the energy I had and channelled it into others rather than myself. I was trying everything possible to make sure that I please people around me. What I did every day was that, before I could engage in any action of some sort, I would think: will this make my family happy? Will this make my teachers happy? Will this make my fellow learners happy? Will this make everyone around me happy? In the process, I never created a space for myself, knowing whether what I engage in would ultimately make myself happy was not even part of my thinking. Indeed, I invested all my energy and efforts into getting praises from everyone around, which I got. What I was thinking was: as long as everyone around me could be happy about this, then I was satisfied. Unfortunately, how what makes others appreciate me made me feel was not something that I ever gave myself time to think about. As a result, I was in bondage, deeply inclined to getting the approval of people in whatever I engaged in. As a result, I did not put aside time to think about my needs, my capabilities and my aspirations.

The worst thing is that in the journey, I developed another character that gradually became my personality. Just because I won everyone's favour, I started regarding myself as better than everyone around me. The way I described greatness was to me kind of astounding. I do not know how you describe greatness but this is how I described it. Greatness to me was when one was in everyone's good books, when everyone relied on that person for answers, when you were seen as someone who has it all; when you were seen as someone who will have it all. It disturbs me to think that I ended up feeling that I am the only person that planet earth needed. I regarded myself as having all the answers. I felt I did not need anyone's opinion or input in whatever I did because after all, I thought that there was nothing good that could come from anyone except from me. This was an arrogant attitude and pride I continued to live with for the period when I was at Bosabethu and eventually later in life.

That attitude was the worst thing that brought me where I am today. I completed my Grade 12, and got a number of scholarships towards studying Medicine at one university. It felt very good to leave home and go to a totally different environment. From the first day, life at the university has been so amazing, in the residences; many people who were accommodated, lecture halls, lecturers themselves, well-resourced laboratories, library and many more other things that were so exciting and new to me. We went through the orientation period which was also exciting, fulfilling and making one to look forward to the actual lectures in the lecture rooms. During that time, I tried to make friends with other newcomers but I did not enjoy their company at all. Topics in their conversations were to me way below my level of thinking. Ultimately, I decided and preferred to be just by myself. As a result, I was spending the best of my time just by myself and I enjoyed my company.

The actual lectures commenced and eventually, the time for handing in our first assignments. That was when things started getting out of hand. To my surprise, for the first time in my life, I got 14% in my Chemistry assignment. I could not stand that, I was so crushed, so shuttered, so hurt and so disappointed that I did not want anyone to see my marks. As I quietly sat on a chair in that lecture room, I was listening to other students sharing their marks and laughing at themselves. They were revealing their marks from 10% to 47%. To my surprise, they were laughing. I asked myself: but why do they have to crack jokes about this? Are they used to this? This was what clouded my thinking at that time. Unfortunately, I was not able to get the answers to all the questions I had about how their reaction was towards the shameful low marks they had obtained in the assignment. I then decided to leave the lecture room and went out as I waited for the Mathematics lecture. I did exactly that, went outside, very far from that noisy Chemistry lecture room.

The Mathematics lecture started and the lecturer gave us group assignment topics. The group that I was in decided to work out the assignment in the evening. We went to the library in the evening as agreed. As we were brainstorming what we wanted to put down, there was a certain boy by the name of Barbrain who dominated the whole session. We had our group chairperson and the secretary. The dominating Barbrain was not one of them. However, Barbrain was contributing significantly towards discussions and I was becoming irritated. But, it looked like other group members were surprised and impressed at his contributions. I was able to notice this because they kept on asking him for clarity on the things he was stating. I did not participate at all, although I was with them, I was so reserved and whenever I wanted to make a contribution, I thought of how disappointed my parents are going to be about my first Chemistry marks.

I felt so bad that I hardly concentrated on what the group was busy with. As discussions continued, I decided to contribute what I read on the topic under discussion. It took me some time to make some contribution because as always I thought, would they accept my contribution? What would happen if my contribution could be regarded as senseless? I was so afraid to be regarded as a fool because I was always the best where I came from. Therefore, the thought of losing that prestige in front of other students made me sick. Another thing that preoccupied my mind was when I heard them picking up challenges as they were proceeding with their discussion. I was quiet sure that I had all the answers to what they were struggling with. I knew my input would save them from the confusion. I was specifically asked to make an input because they said I was completely silent throughout the discussions. That nearly made me contribute, however, I decided to withhold my input. I withheld it because I thought that I would rather keep it to myself than share it with them so that they would notice that I was better off, ready for the test. Indeed, I kept what I knew to myself. In my opinion, spending the late hours of that day in a library was just a waste of time because I did not benefit from the contributions made by other group members because I thought that would make them think that I was desperate.

At last, they managed to complete the task at hand. I became aware that they had completed what they were supposed to do. I was asked to write down my student number on the cover page that had student numbers of all group members. I did that and we ultimately left. The time for us to write our first

Mathematics test came. The test was so challenging and everything that I knew was not even in the test. Even the aspect I did not want to clarify to the group because I had thought we would get in the test was not there. It was challenging.

The next day the lecturer came with our scripts. Before handing out our outcomes, he started by cautioning us that he wanted to congratulate a number of students who performed extraordinarily well in the test. He indicated that during his five-year tenure as a lecturer, we were the first group that managed to obtain high marks in the first test. My heart was thumping in my throat. As he was congratulating us, he also stated that few of us did not do well and he encouraged them to work harder with others and not to give up. I knew which category to align myself with; however, I was so scared, and afraid to face reality. So the thought of being counted amongst those who performed well was unimaginable. I listened to him, thought about it until he started giving us our scripts.

Most of my group members were the first to get their scripts before I could get mine. They were so excited with their marks, they got distinctions. They indicated that many of the questions in the test were the ones that they discussed during their group task. They were thanking Barbrain, the student who dominated the group trying to clarify the concepts that they were struggling with that night. In my mind I knew that I did not even bother listening that night. Could it be that the lecturer was preparing us for the test? That started making sense and ultimately, I discovered that indeed, the lecturer wanted us to help one another. The worst thing was, I discovered that the boy who was dominating the discussion was in his second year. He was repeating that course. It was at that time that I nearly regretted my attitude on that night; however, I told myself that I would also pass and learn these things myself without the assistance of anyone. I told myself that I would rather ask the lecturer for help whenever there was something I wanted clarity on rather than to ask my fellow students.

Finally, my script came, yet another shock of the moment. I didn't know how I should react as all eyes were on me as I was handed my script. I had to hide my feelings so that no one could notice the hurt and frustration. I did exactly that, stared at my script, kept a jovial face and put my script in my bag. I knew nobody will bother knowing my marks because they were not used to me. It was a disgrace, a shame and a disappointment. All along I thought I was very good in Mathematics. I received academic awards for my entire High school period. What I was seeing was indescribable, it was difficult for me to handle, especially because 99% of my fellow students were celebrating their marks. Unfortunately, for me, it was yet another setback. Once again, I started thinking about how my parents are going to react and that made me feel even more desperate. The thought that clouded my mind at that moment was how I was going to tell my parents that I got 6% in my first Mathematics test.

I quietly sat on my chair because the lecturer made us settle down for him to introduce another topic. He gave us an outline of what we needed to learn about the topic and, once again, he told us to go and discuss the topics in our groups. We were told that we were expected to make a PowerPoint presentation on the topics that would be allocated to us on the day. That meant that we had to go and prepare all topics because we did not know the one that would be allocated to us on the day. I was so hurt, I wanted to work by myself, I did not want to be part of the group. I never worked in groups before. I used to ask teachers to work by myself as others were told to work in groups and I was forever afforded that opportunity.

Being forced to work in groups got into me and I told myself that I would ask to be granted permission to work by myself. I went straight to the lecturer and asked, unfortunately, he told me that I should work alone and thereafter go and discuss what I found with my group members so that they could learn from me and, in the same way, I could also learn from them. I was so disappointed when I left his office because he was telling me to do what I did not want to do. I did not want to share my knowledge and make people to benefit from what I know. Unfortunately, he told me that was the only system that he used with his students because it worked well for him and them. I totally did not agree with him because what worked for him and other students might not work for me.

I was so bored that day; my head was heavy as I was leaving that block of lecturers' offices. I told myself that I was going straight to my room to sleep before I could open my books. On my way to the room, I went past a certain lady who remarked about my hairstyle and wanted to know where I had it done. I had to stop and walk with her as I was trying to tell her that I did it at home. She then introduced herself to me which I also did. Her name was Olwethu. We found out that we were coming from the same province and she then wanted to know where I was staying. Although I did not want to tell her, I had to do it because she was so friendly. After showing her my room, she insisted that I have to go and see hers as well. Again, I did not want to, but I had to because I thought that was being rude.

We then went to her room; it was a well-furnished room. Olwethu had everything; a heavily loaded double door fridge, a stove, a well-mounted 81cm LED TV, leather sofas, an oak study table with a black arm rest office leather chair. She had everything, as I looked at her windows; snow white curtains were on the wall. The curtains matched the duvet and pillows she had laid on the bed. I was so surprised, I felt like I was in a five-star hotel because in the bathroom she had white towels and a white morning gown that was hanging on its rail. I was so startled that I ended up asking her about how she managed to take care of her white linen. She told me that she had two sets of the same linen and that she takes one set to the laundry every week. Then I thought to myself; this one must be coming from a wealthy family.

Olwethu realised that I was so amazed and she told me that I could also get the same things if I so desired. I then briefly started telling her that my family could hardly afford to pay my tuition fees. Immediately, she told me that she also came from a very poor family but she had to break that chain of poverty herself. I then became interested in knowing how she managed to do all that.

CHAPTER 5

I waited patiently for her as she went to her kitchenette and brought juice and snacks. We then sat on a sofa, and she started telling me how she managed to have everything that she had. Unfortunately, what I thought about where she got her possessions was not what I heard. Olwethu told me that she suffered a lot during her first year at the university because of her disadvantaged family background. Fortunately, during her second year, she was lucky to find a man by the name of Phemelo who was very rich and has since been taking care of her. She told me that the man has even went to negotiate lobola for her but her family refused and asked him to wait until she finishes her studies. She then told me that if I really love what she had I should wait a bit in her room and meet the person behind all what she had. She told me that Phemelo will be coming to her room in an hour's time.

Suddenly, there was a knock at the door and two gentlemen came in. I was then introduced to them. It was Phemelo and Thenjiwe. They brought plastics full of groceries which they helped packing in the fridge and the drawers. As I was looking at every move they were making, I immediately felt attracted to Thenjiwe. He was tall, hefty, a bit dark in complexion and very handsome. He appeared to be so humble and respectful. He was in his sporty outfit and a cap which he immediately took off as they were entering Olwethu's room. The atmosphere in the room was so peaceful and full of hope for the future. The two guys immediately told us that they wanted to watch a soccer match. We stayed and watched soccer with them. It was getting late; I knew I had to go to the library for a Maths discussion. However, the marks I got and the thought of staying with all group members made me decide to stay over and watch the soccer match with them. I stayed and watched soccer for the very first time in my life. At that time, I was not concentrating on the soccer match at all. Instead, I was playing games on my cell phone. Phemelo and Thenjiwe were drinking juice as they were watching the game.

During half time, Thenjiwe decided to come and sit closer to me. He innocently held my right hand and with a smile, he simply told me that I am beautiful. That felt very good, but I did not want to show that to anyone. I just giggled and appreciated the compliment. The soccer team that the two guys loved and supported lost the game and they were so hurt that they decided to leave. But before they left, Thenjiwe asked for my cell phone number. I gave it to him with the hope that he will call me. It was already late when I also decided to go back to my room. I could not go to the library at that time and therefore decided to notify the group leader that I was not well. But, for some time, I stayed with Olwethu until I decided to go back to my room. She packed some of the goodies that were brought by the two guys and gave me.

That night, I hardly slept. Thenjiwe was all over me. The feeling I had was so deep. I was in love with Thenjiwe. Remember, he only took my number and I never bothered to have his. I hated myself for not having thought of asking for his number. Little did I know that the feeling was mutual. As I was struggling to fall asleep, I saw an unsaved number calling. The caller introduced himself as Thenjiwe and he asked if he could come to see me because he was struggling to sleep. I told him it was late and then he thanked me for having taken his call, asked for my room number and promised to call back the following day.

The next day by 7am, Thenjiwe called to ask as to what time he could come over. I then told him to come at 10am because I had a morning lecture. After the lecture, he came over in his luxury car. Unlike yesterday, he was in his formal attire, a white shirt and a sky blue tie. He was so handsome that I kept asking myself if he was not a playboy. He requested that I should go with him because he wanted to submit documents somewhere. I agreed and went with him. On our way, he said nothing about his interest in me or anything along those lines. He was only bringing general topics that we engaged in, that felt very uncomfortable at first.

We arrived at the offices where he wanted to drop his documents and he parked his car on the CEO's bay. That he could be the CEO did not even cross my mind. He offered that I should accompany him and I agreed. On our way to the office, he was greeting everyone we met with great respect; starting with the security guard at the door. I was just watching and silently appreciating his humility. He took me to what I thought was his office, only to discover whilst I was in there that it was a boardroom. We sat as if we were in a meeting and a woman brought snacks and drinks. He then introduced himself in a more detailed way. His family background, his upbringing and where he was at the moment. It is at that time that I became aware that he was the CEO of that very big company.

I felt out of place, but he made me feel at ease. I also introduced myself to him. He told me that he was married and had two boys but, unfortunately his wife died of breast cancer two months before and he was still mourning her death. He told me that he got attracted to me immediately after laying eyes on me in Olwethu's room but he did not want to show it. At that moment, I found it very difficult to deny the affection I had towards him. He stood from where he was seated and came to hug me and promised to take care of me. He then took me back to the university and promised to visit in the evening. Indeed, he came, and spent quality time with me. As we were talking, he told me that I should not be surprised because he was not going to make any sexual advances to me because he still had three months remaining to mourn his wife.

Thenjiwe and I became very close; we spent most of our free time together. He was such a good man that I never thought existed in the entire universe. The mourning period expired and he invited me to the cleansing ceremony. I went to the ceremony with Olwethu. We were warmly welcomed by the family and his two sons. To our surprise, the whole family wanted to know who Mmakgabo was as they were greeting us. Like how he once proposed to me, the ceremony made him send his uncle and aunt to my family. My family welcomed them and we got married. He bought a new beautiful house for me not very far from his old home where he left his two sons.

I was continuing with my studies but I was totally not doing well. The poor performance was persisting in most of the courses and that was discouraging me. I even regretted registering for that course thinking that maybe if I had chosen a different one like Physiotherapy or Radiography I would have performed better. I thought about this because I knew that, despite my poor performance, medicine was not what I loved. It was my teachers and my parents who insisted that I should follow medicine; I just did not want to let them down. As a result of my very poor performance in MBChB, I withheld my results from both my husband and my family. Whenever they were asking how I was doing, I would lie to them and tell them that studies were going well. My husband advised me to take contraceptives until I finish my studies and I agreed. He bought a luxury car for me so that I could be able to travel to the university. On my own, I decided that I was not going to take contraceptives and I fell pregnant. I told my husband that I was surprised as he was because I was religiously taking my pill. That year I did not register at the university and I gave birth to a boy. He hired a child-minder and a housemaid for me. All what I did at home was to feed and play with the child. The following year my husband gave me money to register at the university. I agreed but rather used the money to buy clothes. Every day I would pretend to be going to the university. The thought of me working with other students was distressing me. The thought of me getting poor marks was discouraging me. The thought of me being seen to be struggling with my studies was haunting and worrying me.

The thought of me seeing students that I started with in higher levels was upsetting me. For the whole year, I was living that lie, I would pretend to be studying at night whilst I was only doing my nails or glued on WhatsApp. Once again, I decided to skip a pill and became pregnant. This time my husband was not happy but he had to accept that the pregnancy was another mistake. He was so disappointed because he so much wanted me to finish my studies. I gave birth to another boy and my husband was very happy.

Years went by and I never initiated going back to the university. We were very happy as a family and Thenjiwe's two sons often came for a visit. My own sons grew at an alarming speed and before we knew it, they were due for a crèche and later for school. My husband was always suggesting that I had to go and finish my degree but I kept on saying I would go and enquire. One day, on a Wednesday, Thenjiwe's sons decided to come and have dinner with us like they always did. That day marked a turning point of all the luxury I had. As we were all at the dinner table, Sthembiso (Thenjiwe's eldest son) asked about my studies. Everyone was staring at me waiting for my response. I immediately told him that I had since put my studies on hold because of my pregnancy. He followed it up and asked about the progress I had made.

At that moment I started feeling sweat on my brow but managed to tell him that I was in my third year. He then suggested that I should start enquiring and registering so that I can be able to finish my degree. My husband and his second son, Sephiwe, supported him. As if that was not enough, Sthembiso then offered to make an enquiry through the internet on my behalf because he was also studying at the same university. My two sons were not there because my husband had decided to put them at a boarding school and they were only coming home on Fridays and leaving on Monday morning.

I immediately told Sthembiso not to worry because I had already planned to do the enquiry myself. He then agreed but told me that I should let him know whenever I come across challenges and we agreed. That day I did not sleep, I was trying to figure out what my next move would be and I did not have a clue. The thought of going back to the university was not going to work for me because at that time, I had told myself that I was not coping and I was not going to give in to group discussion. I immediately decided to change my attitude towards the boys and claimed that they were rude and spoilt. My husband was so surprised and promised to talk to the boys. He did not know that I was blaming the innocent boys because I was hiding something from him.

One day we were having our dinner as always when we heard the doorbell. It was my husband's boys, Sthembiso and Sephiwe. I immediately became very frantic and agitated. I told my husband that he should not allow them to come into our house. My husband begged for my tolerance but I insisted that I would leave and give them some space and would only come back when they had gone because I was in no way ready to sit with them. I did exactly that, my husband was so frustrated and did not know what to do. That became a norm; whenever the boys wanted to come I would excuse myself. My husband was so worried and he tried hard to apologise for whatever wrong they did to me but I did not listen. Years went by and the boys decided not to come and visit us anymore. Instead, my husband was visiting them whenever he was missing them. That did not fare well with my husband but he told me that he was only tolerating it because he loved me and did not want to hurt me.

It was on one Saturday afternoon when we went to a restaurant for lunch with our boys. As we were eating, Mdudusi, our eldest son started asking me whether I enjoyed staying at home all by myself when other women go to work. She went on and said she remember me telling them that I was studying to be a doctor. I immediately became offended and told her not to ask that again. I lost my appetite and decided to go wait for them in the car. My husband was surprised at my reaction towards the young boy and he started recalling the time when Sthembiso offered to help with the re-registration enquiry. Pieces of the puzzle started coming together and he decided to follow it up himself without telling me. We then went home and my husband told me to register. Once again, I lied; I told him that I did and he gave me the money that I requested. I did not know that he gave Sthembiso my student number to make an enquiry as well.

The following year, I pretended to be going to the university every day. My husband gave me all the money that I needed for tuition and travelling. He gave me pocket money, took my car for car wash and filled the petrol tank every week. He was so patient with me whenever I was unable to provide my academic record. The whole thing lasted for three years. I lived a lie, when they thought I was going to the university, I was going to a Casino, to the Cinema and sometimes to the different malls every day. Sometimes I would just lock myself in the visitors' room and pretended not to be at home. I did not have a good relationship with the two ladies who were working for us and our garden man. That time I thought that they so much loved dragging their feet as they were doing their chores but the truth was that I did not like them because we were paying them a lot of money as compared to other helpers.

As a result, they were not able to trace my movements. I would leave and come back as I pleased. They were not opening the visitors' room because I had told them not to and to clean it only when I told them. I continued like that, I did not have peace of mind. I tried for so long to tell my husband the truth, but I failed. One day I decided to go to the casino, as I was busy playing; there was a certain man by the name of Tshegofatxo that I was already used to. We greeted each other as always and that day we kept each other's company. We became very close and one day we ended up in bed together. Things between me and Tshegofatxo continued like that and I started losing interest in my husband. I started denying my husband conjugal rights pretending to be ill and he was so patient with me.

One day I told him that I had an evening lesson and I asked to sleep with my friend at the university because I was also having a morning lecturer the following day. He agreed, and I knew that I was seeing Tshegofatxo that night. That happened and I did that more often. Unfortunately, I became pregnant and I was so scared to tell my husband. After having discovered that I was pregnant, one day my husband decided to follow me as I was pretending to be going to the university. He was using someone else's car and I could not notice that the car was following me. As usual, I went to the Casino where I was meeting Tshegofatxo. We went to the lodge as always and booked a room. I don't know how my husband did it but after three hours, he came knocking at our room and shouted: "room service". I then jumped from the bed to the door, to my surprise; it was my husband who was knocking. I was so in shock, Tshegofatxo heard me screaming and came running, he asked who the person was and I told him that it was my husband. My husband was so calm and quiet; he did not say a word but only asked for my car keys and my ring. He then left. I was so much in shock but slept over at the lodge with Tshegofatxo because we had already booked for the night.

The next morning was Friday and I knew my boys were coming home. I was so scared to face my husband. But I summoned courage in the evening and took a taxi home. I knocked and he came to the gate with my boys. He denied me access to my house. As we were standing at the gate, he showed me my academic record that I have never written a single examination and the horrible assignment results that I got. My sons were quiet, staring at me with hate, and I realised that he had already told them everything. That he wasted money on me for three years thinking I was studying while I was sleeping with another man. Eventually, they turned their back and went back to the house. I was crying for forgiveness but nobody listened.

I stood at the gate, thinking they could change their minds and open the gate for me. But, I realised that the longer I stayed there, the darker it was becoming. I then decided to call Tshegofatxo and told him my predicament. He ordered me to catch a taxi and gave me direction to where he was staying. I did that, to my surprise, the taxi took me to an informal settlement. That was exactly where he was staying. A smelly shack was his home. I had to spend the night there. It was then that I started realising that he did not own a car, he did not have money and he was repeatedly putting on the same clothes. I always used my cards whenever we needed cash or accommodation. I started realising that I was always paying for the lodge. I did not realise that then because I had a lot of money that I had to spend. Fortunately, my husband did not take my bank cards and I knew I still had the cash I was saving to last me for some time.

I did not sleep that night. The noise outside was just unbearable because it was something I was not used to. The following morning, I decided to catch a taxi again and go back to ask for forgiveness. It was my youngest son, Lesiba, who saw me at the gate and he yelled at me telling me to go back to the man that made me to lie and neglect his father. His brother Mdudusi also showed up and helped him to chase me away like a dog. My husband heard the noise they were making and came out only to find that I was in that commotion. He then ordered the boys to go inside the house and he just stared at me for some time as I was pleading for forgiveness. Without saying a word, he also went back to the house. For hours, I stood at the gate and later decided to go back to Tshegofatxo.

Tshegofatxo welcomed me but he had nothing. We relied on the money I had until all my savings became dry. We started starving; we sometimes went to bed hungry. Tshegofatxo was trying to do garden jobs but people were not paying him on time. One day, I decided to go back home and ask my parents to go to my husband to plead for my forgiveness. On my arrival at home, before I could even saw my mother, my father saw me and chased me out of the house like a dog. My relatives and neighbours were called and they all mocked me to their satisfaction. They called me names; a butterfly, a prostitute, all sort of dirty names. I then went back to Tshegofatxo and we stayed there together starving. During my ninth month, I got ill and was taken to a nearby public hospital. Unfortunately, I got a miscarriage. As if that was not enough, two months thereafter, Tshegofatxo became very ill.

He did not want to go to hospital, he was very ill. One day, he gave me the cell numbers of a certain man and ordered me to call that man. I called the man and that man promised to come. As I was doing laundry outside after having given Tshegofatxo something to eat, a certain man arrived at our shack. He introduced himself as Mr Mbhilinyana, I then went with him inside of the shack and we found Tshegofatxo's body, he was dead. I was in pain and miserable. He was the only thing I was left with on earth. To my surprise, Mr Mbhilinyana did not show any sign of shock regarding Tshegofatxo's sudden death. He looked at me and said: Are you the woman who infected him with HIV/AIDS?

I was so surprised and did not understand what he was talking about. Mr Mbhilinyana then suggested that he was calling Tshegofatxo's wife because we could not remove his body ourselves without her consent. I did not know that he had a wife, I was startled. Tshegogatxo had been such a closed book to me, which is what I said to myself. Within an hour a car was parked outside and a woman and three boys came in. On their arrival, they checked the dead body and immediately turned to me. The boys started hitting me so badly blaming me for having killed their father after having ripped him of his pension money. The woman they came with and Mr Mbhilinyana tried to stop them but they did not succeed. I was badly hit and bled terribly. I then fell and fainted. When I woke up, I was in that hospital where I had a miscarriage and nurses told me that I was brought by an ambulance.

After three days, I was discharged and had bandages and bruises all over my body. I then decided to go to Tshegofatxo's shack because it was my new home. To my surprise, when I arrived, there was nothing. The shack was demolished and everything taken. As I stood there in shock, a certain woman started a commotion: "the witch is back, come let us deal with her; she killed our neighbour but has the guts to come back here"! I then saw people coming with big knifes and slashes. With my bandages, they hit me so badly that I lost consciousness. Once again, I found myself in the same hospital for the third time now. When I was discharged, I decided to go to my husband. I knew that he would not love to see me in that state. I did that, unfortunately, I found new owners and they told me they had moved a month before. People I found did not even know where the previous owners of the house went because the house was bought through agents.

I then decided to go back home. I did not have money; I had to beg for food and transport money. When I arrived at home, my mother did not welcome me at all. The same way as my father did, she also chased me away like a dog; being in that medical state. She told me that I made a joke of her in the whole neighbourhood; I was the girl that she trusted, the girl who was so brilliant and intelligent at school, the girl who was better than all the girls and boys but decided to make her life a misery. As my mother was saying all the unforgiving and punitive words, I realised how I disappointed her. I knew what I did and I hated myself for that, however, I had forgiven myself because I realised where everything went wrong.

It was at that time that I started realising that people around you will always put pressure on you. People around you want you when you have it all, people around you do not want to be associated with a failure, and people around you will always try to make you become who you are not. Another thing that I realised was that, people around you will never bother asking the side of your story for them to understand what you are going through. They will only judge you with what they see with their naked eye. They will only judge you against the standards they have set for you.

My mother then went into the house and brought a bunch of keys. She gave me the key and told me that they were the keys for my grandmother's shack. She told me to go and stay there and to never come back to her house because she did not want to be seen in my company. I took the keys, and off I went. This is the shack that we are sitting in Lebone. I stay here by myself, I am struggling, and I rely on hand-outs. I hate the title that Bosabethu Secondary School had given me, that I am an intelligent girl. I think that label is the one that brought me here. If it was not for it, I would have found it easy to appreciate and learn from inputs that were made by other students at the university. If it was not for the label, I would have found it very easy to work together with other students. If it was not for the label, I would have found it very easy to tell my husband that I was not performing well so that I could change courses and did something else. The label made me to keep on to my parents' dreams of becoming a medical doctor; it made me to live a lie, to become an alien in my own skin. I hate that label Lebone, I hate it so much. I have been crushed and shuttered by that label. At that time, Mmakgabo drank water as a sign to show that she had finished telling me what she wanted to tell me.

It was already late; I heard everything that I wanted to hear. Even more than what I had thought. Although I did not enjoy listening to her misery, I was so motivated. I was so motivated that, although I had never received an academic award, I was no longer going to be discouraged and think that I will not make it at tertiary institutions because even those who got all the merits and awards sometimes do not make it. My last thought was to convince myself that my attitude towards life; and not what other people see me for, was the only thing that would determine how far I would go in life.

Mmakgabo then stood and walked me out of her house. She then said to me: Lebone, go back and bounce back. Fight for your life, fight a good fight. Do not fight because you want to please people around you. Fight because you want to accomplish the dreams that you have set for yourself, not to supress the pressure that you are being put under and surrounded by. Rest assured, if you can continue making sure that you live life for yourself, set goals for yourself and work very hard and collaboratively with other learners, you will surely accomplish your dreams. Good luck Lebone!

I then went home, happier than ever, ready to fight a good fight, ready to chase my dreams. The thought of me being regarded as stupid was expunged; I was so full of energy and all thanks went to Mmakgabo. This is what made me to decide to write this letter to Bosabethu Secondary School. I wanted to encourage all learners who go to school every day all year round and do not get a single award that: an award does not determine their success in life; their success in life depends on their attitude towards life; they must work hard and not put themselves under pressure to be appreciated and to please the society; all children, with their different capabilities have all that it takes to become successful; they must never allow society to dictate otherwise because if they do, they will get tired along the way; they should not allow anybody, be it a teacher, parents or any member of the community to make them feel inferior; they are talented, unique and powerful in their own way; they need to appreciate and love themselves for who they are and what they are capable of; they need to focus and work hard so that they can be able to improve and learn more every day; they must never be tempted to measure their capabilities by the number of awards, they receive; they must go out and dig for the precious gold that has been put aside for them in different locations and avenues, specifically for them. I wanted to make them aware that: if they start working very hard in all areas they want to venture, before they know it, they will start seeing the gold they had been digging and what they must do with the gold is to burn and polish it to eventually become the product they aspire for. In doing that, their diverse products from the gold will be put together and make the world a better place for all to live in.

Lastly, I say to all learners in schools: let me do my part, you also have to do your part, and together let us share and teach each other how we managed to come out with our different products. This world belongs to us, to all of us, not the chosen few that are being chosen for whatever reason. This world is such a tiny little space that we all have to own and take responsibility for whatever happens in it. Let us stop feeling comfortable in the passenger's seat and all assume the driver's seat to make it a better place that we will all ultimately become proud of. Our success in this world depends solely on what we choose and decide to do with our lives, not on what other people think of us.

MY FINAL REMARKS FROM THE BOTTOM OF MY HEART

To Bosabethu Secondary School: if you believe that all children have talents worth celebrating, why are you not making an effort to celebrate all of those talents? Children have unique talents and they all need recognition. All of them need to be recognized for their talents. They all need to be encouraged in areas that they are passionate about and have strength in. Review how you award your learners and in the process, guard against discriminatory practices.

To teachers of Bosabethu Secondary School: do you sometimes take time and reflect on the damage you are causing on children's self-esteem? Your subjective judgement on who and what has to be awarded does more harm to the children than what you may realise. It is important to make all of them to realise that their various talents are equally important and valued. When you start to subjectively categorise their talents by awarding some while leaving out others, you are indirectly telling others that their talents amount to nothing and are not worth celebrating.

Furthermore, you need to reflect on your schooling years. Think about how you were limited to perform certain tasks as a learner while at the same time labelled as bad in other tasks. Think of the teaching methods your teachers were using which ultimately made you not to get distinctions in either one or all the subjects you were doing. Based on your schooling experience, when you plan lessons for your class, think of the diversity of learners in your class and make sure that you plan for all of them. As you present lessons in your class, think of the diversity of learners in your class and make sure that you use teaching strategies that cater for all of them. And, when you assess learners in your class, make sure that you use different assessment methods that cater for the diversity of learners that you have in your class. In that way, you will start realising that all children have the capacity when they are being appropriately supported. As a result, you will start recognizing their various talents and the need to celebrate all of them.

To parents of Bosabethu Secondary School: why do you put pressure on your children to get awards at the school? Why do you allow the school to discriminate learners? Are you aware that all children can learn when given the appropriate support? Do you know that these children have different intelligences and they need to be supported differently by yourselves and teachers? Why do you allow the school to award some of your children while leaving out others? The one-size-fits all teaching approaches that are being used by teachers in classrooms do not cater for the diversity of learners. Unfortunately, these traditional approaches that they use are the ones that teachers are comfortable with because most of them are not ready to take an effort to explore other teaching strategies that cater for the diversity of learners.

You cannot continue to allow schools to discriminate between your children. You cannot allow schools to continue labelling and classifying learners. All children deserve to be celebrated, loved, cherished and motivated at the school. When some children are being singled out, relationships among children get disrupted and that often result in pride, selfishness and jealousy. An element of togetherness which is a virtue that children need to develop for them to be able to be part of the community in future also becomes tarnished. Lastly, I want to challenge you: let the policy on prize-giving ceremonies of Bosabethu Secondary School be reviewed. As you review the policy, make sure that no children become discriminated on any account, instead, make sure that the different talents and various capabilities of all children at the school became valued celebrated.

From your Grade 12 learner

Lebone Seghayi